GALE
CENGAGE Learning

Short Stories for Students, Volume 1

STAFF

Kathleen Wilson, *Editor*

Tim Akers, Pamela S. Dear, David M. Galens, Jeffrey W. Hunter, Dan Jones, John D. Jorgenson, Marie Lazzari,
Jerry Moore, Deborah A. Stanley, Diane Telgen, Polly Vedder, Thomas Wiloch, *Contributing Editors*

Jeff Chapman, *Programmer/Analyst*

Greg Barnhisel, Stephan Dziemianowicz, Tim Engles, Mary Beth Folia, Christopher Giroux, Cynthia Hallett, Karen
Holleran, Jennifer Hicks, Logan Hill, Heidi Johnson, Tamara Kendig, David Kippen, Maryanne Kocis, Rena Korb,
Kim Long, Harvey Lynch, Thomas March, Carl Mowery, Rober~ ~mont-Marton, Trudy R

D1334331

Judy Sobeloff, Michael Sonkowsky, Anne Trubek, Julianne White, Janet Witalec, *Contributing Writers*

Susan Trosky, *Permissions Manager*
Kim Smilay, *Permissions Specialist*
Sarah Chesney, *Permissions Associate*
Steve Cusack, Kelly A. Quin, *Permissions Assistants*

Victoria Cariappa, *Research Team Leader*
Michele LaMeau, Barbara McNeil, Maureen Richards, *Research Specialists*
Laura C. Bissey, Julia C. Daniel, Tamara C. Nott, Tracie Richardson,
Norma Sawaya, Cheryl L. Warnock, *Research Associates*

Mary Beth Trimper, *Production Director*
Shanna Heilveil, *Production Assistant*

Cynthia Baldwin, *Production Design Manager*
Pamela A. E. Galbreath, *Senior Art Director*

Barbara J. Yarrow, *Graphic Services Manager*
Pamela Reed, *Photography Coordinator*
Randy Bassett, *Image Database Supervisor*

Copyright © 1997
Gale Research
835 Penobscot Building
Detroit, MI 48226-4094

ISBN 0-7876-1690-7
ISSN 1092-7735

Printed in the United States of America.
10 9 8 7 6 5 4 3 2

The Yellow Wallpaper

Charlotte Perkins Gilman 1892

Introduction

"The Yellow Wallpaper," first published in 1892 in the *New England Magazine*, is largely considered Charlotte Perkins Gilman's best work of short fiction. The story is a first-person account of a young mother's mental deterioration and is based on Gilman's own experiences with postpartum depression. Like Gilman, the unnamed protagonist of the story is advised, based on medical theories of the time, to abstain from any and all physical activity and intellectual stimulation. She is not allowed to read, write, or even see her new baby. To carry out this treatments, the woman's husband takes her to a country house where she is kept in a former nursery decorated with yellow wallpaper.

Gilman initially had difficulties getting "The Yellow Wallpaper" published. Horace Scudder of *The Atlantic* refused to print it, stating "I could not forgive myself if I made others as miserable as I have made myself!" Eventually, "The Yellow Wallpaper" began to win converts, and American writer William Dean Howells included it in his *The Great Modern American Stories: An Anthology* in 1920. Early reviewers generally classified "The Yellow Wallpaper" as a horror story, with most commenting on Gilman's use of Gothic conventions. It was not until Elaine R. Hedges's afterward to a 1973 edition of the story that "The Yellow Wallpaper" began receiving scholarly attention. Most modern commentators now interpret the story as a feminist indictment of society's subjugation of women and praise its compelling characterization, complex symbolism, and thematic depth.

Author Biography

Charlotte Perkins Gilman was born in 1860 in Hartford, Connecticut, to Frederick Beecher Perkins, a noted librarian and magazine editor, and his wife, Mary Fritch Perkins. Although Gilman's father frequently left the family for long periods during her childhood and eventually divorced his wife in 1869, he directed Gilman's early education, emphasizing study in the sciences and history. During his absences, Perkins left his wife and children with his relatives. This brought Gilman into frequent contact with her independent and reform-minded great-aunts: Harriet Beecher Stowe, an abolitionist and author of *Uncle Tom's Cabin;* Catherine Beecher, the prominent advocate of "domestic feminism"; and Isabella Beecher Hooker, an ardent suffragist. Their influence—and the example of her mother's own self-reliance—were instrumental in developing Gilman's feminist convictions and desire to effect social reform. Early in her life, Gilman displayed the independence she later advocated for women: she insisted on remuneration for her household chores, and later she paid her mother room and board while supporting herself as a teacher and as a commercial artist.

At twenty-four, she married Charles Walter Stetson, who was also an artist. Following the birth of their daughter in 1884, Gilman suffered a severe depression. She consulted the noted neurologist S.

Weir Mitchell, who prescribed his "rest-cure": complete bed rest and limited intellectual activity. Gilman credited this experience with driving her "near the borderline of utter mental ruin." The rest-cure served as the basis for Gilman's best known work, "The Yellow Wallpaper." She removed herself from Mitchell's care, and later, attributing her emotional problems in part to the confines of marriage, left her husband.

After her separation, Gilman moved to California, where she helped edit feminist publications, assisted in the planning of the California Women's Congresses of 1894 and 1895, and was instrumental in founding the Women's Peace Party. She spent several years lecturing in the United States and England on women's rights and on labor reform, and in 1898 she published *Women and Economics: A Study of the Economic Relation between Men and Women as a Factor in Social Evolution*. In 1900, she married George Houghton Gilman, who was supportive of her intense involvement in social reform. From 1909 through 1916 Gilman published a monthly journal, *The Forerunner*, for which she wrote nearly all of the copy. In 1935, having learned that she was suffering from inoperable cancer, Gilman took her life. She wrote in a final note that "when one is assured of unavoidable and imminent death, it is the simplest of human rights to choose a quick and easy death in place of a slow and horrible one."

Plot Summary

"The Yellow Wallpaper" opens with the musings of an unnamed woman. She, her husband John, their newborn baby, and her sister-in-law have rented a summer house. The narrator is suffering from postpartum depression, and the summer house will function as a place for her to get better. The doctor has prescribed a rest cure of quiet and solitude, with an emphasis on avoiding any form of mental stimulation like reading or writing. The woman notes that the room in which she is staying seems to be geared more for incarceration than rehabilitation. John classifies her merely as "sick," thereby exhibiting the prevailing attitude of the day, that mental illness in women was not real. Following the doctor's strict orders, he forbids his wife from doing any type of work and does not allow her to see her baby. The narrator believes that work, excitement, and change would do her good, but her opinion does not matter. She would like to write, which is forbidden, and surreptitiously keeping a diary exhausts her, as does trying to oppose her husband. With very little to do, the woman is left to contemplate the ugly yellow wallpaper in the nursery that is coming off the wall in great patches. She begins to trace the pattern of the wallpaper. The woman's narration abruptly ends because her husband is coming.

The story continues two weeks later when the narrator is able to write again. Even though she feels it might help relieve some of her tension, she generally gives in to her husband's desire that she not write. She has been feeling terribly depressed, but John says her case is not serious. He does not think her suffering amounts to anything more than "nervousness." He laughs at her hatred for the wallpaper, and though she wants him to repaper the room, he refuses to give in to her "fancies." When the narrator claims to have seen people walking on the path by the house, he cautions her that giving in to her imagination will overexcite her. The woman starts to examine the wallpaper, noticing how the patterns form "eyes" that seem to be staring at her. When the sunlight shines in a certain way, she sees a figure skulking behind the pattern of the wallpaper. Again, the narrator must stop writing, for her sister-in-law, Jennie, is coming up the stairs.

Because the narrator does not seem to be getting better and spends a lot of time crying, John threatens to send her to Weir Mitchell, a doctor who believes even more strongly than himself in rest treatments. The narrator has become fond of the room, perhaps because of the wallpaper. She enjoys lying on her bed, following the patterns in the wallpaper and attempting to trace one of the strands to a conclusion. As she spends all her time in the bedroom, the wallpaper continues to captivate the narrator. She realizes that it knows things about her that no one else does. More alarmingly, the figure she sees in the wallpaper has begun to take shape—that of a woman stooping down and creeping behind the pattern.

One night the narrator tells John that she is getting no better and wants to leave the house, but he refuses, insisting the rest cure will work. She then returns to her examination of the wallpaper. Her diligent attention reveals that there is a front pattern and a back pattern and that at night the front pattern forms bars. The woman in the wallpaper is quiet during the day and more active at night, as is the narrator. The narrator has also grown fearful of John and Jennie, for they seem to be studying the wallpaper as if they want to understand its pattern before she does.

During the last week of their stay, the narrator fakes improved health and spirits when her husband is around but has become completely obsessed with the wallpaper. She constantly notices new facets of the wallpaper: the smell of yellow that creeps through the whole house; a streak along the baseboard encircling the room. She discovers that the woman in the wallpaper shakes the bars of the front pattern as she tries, unsuccessfully, to climb through them. Though she has only two days left in the house, she is determined to get the paper off and thus free the woman inside.

When John is away one evening, she locks the door, throws the keys out the window, and begins peeling the wallpaper. Despite her efforts, however, she cannot remove it all. In her desperation, she considers committing suicide but decides that this would be "improper and might be misconstrued." She begins circling the room, following the pattern of the wallpaper, in essence becoming the woman inside, trapped in an endless maze. John breaks open the door to see his wife creeping along the wall and faints. The narrator only laughs. His slumped body is blocking her path, and she is forced to creep over him each time she circles the room.

Characters

Jennie

Jennie is the narrator's sister-in-law. She helps to take care of the narrator and, more importantly, the narrator's newborn baby. She is described as "a perfect and enthusiastic housekeeper." She represents the nineteenth-century view of the role of women as housekeepers and child rearers.

John

The husband of the unnamed narrator, John is a doctor who believes in the "rest-cure," a treatment developed by real-life neurologist S. Weir Mitchell, for women suffering from hysteria. Therefore, he prescribes complete bed rest, not allowing his wife to do anything. John in many ways treats his wife like a child, calling her his "blessed little goose" and "little girl." The character displays the nineteenth-century attitude that women were to behave demurely and remain within the domestic sphere, aspiring only to be competent mothers and charming wives.

Media Adaptations

- A short film adaptation of "The Yellow Wallpaper" was produced in 1977 by Marie Ashton and is available on videotape through Women Make Movies.

- "The Yellow Wallpaper" was adapted as a television film, produced by the British Broadcasting Company (BBC) for its series "Masterpiece Theatre" in 1989. It was adapted by Maggie Wadey and directed by John Clive.

- "The Yellow Wallpaper" appeared as an audio, book in 1997. Read by Win Phillips, it was produced by Durkin Hayes.

Unnamed protagonist

The unnamed narrator of "The Yellow Wallpaper" is married to John, a doctor, and has just recently had a baby. She suffers from depression, or "nervous prostration," and is confined to a room that used to be a nursery, as a "bed-rest" cure, in a country house that she and her husband are renting for a holiday. While John does not allow her to read, write, or engage in any other type of mental stimulation, she does secretly write in a journal. The story itself is a transcription of these journal entries. Bored and restless, the narrator is driven to distraction by the yellow wallpaper that decorates the room, eventually suffering a complete mental breakdown after imagining that she sees in the wallpaper's pattern women who are trying to escape. Because the narrator is completely dependent on her husband and is allowed no other role than to be a wife and mother, she represents the secondary status of women during the nineteenth century.

"The Yellow Wallpaper" is the story of a woman who suffers from depression. Advised by her husband to rest, the woman becomes obsessed by the yellow wallpaper that decorates the room in which she has been confined.

Role of Women

"The Yellow Wallpaper" examines the role of women in nineteenth-century American society, including the relationship between husbands and wives, the economic and social dependence of women on men, and the repression of female individuality and sexuality. The Victorian Age had a profound impact on the social values in the United States. Victorian values stressed that women were to behave demurely and remain within the domestic sphere. Suffering from postpartum depression after the birth of her son, the protagonist is advised to get complete bed rest by her husband and brother, despite her suggestions that she would like to write and read. While she does secretly write in a journal, it is made clear that her husband is to be the final decision-maker and that she has no role other than to be a charming wife and a competent mother. In fact, John often treats her like a child, calling her his "little girl" and his "blessed little goose." When the narrator has a "real earnest reasonable talk" with John during which she asks him if she can visit some relatives, he does not allow her to go.

Mental Illness

"The Yellow Wallpaper," because of its first-person description of mental illness, is also considered a work of psychological fiction. In the story Gilman addresses such themes as madness, depression, despair, and self-worth by presenting a realistic and shocking account of the stages of mental breakdown. Because the narrator has nothing to do to occupy herself and because she has no say in her treatment, she comes to project all of her pent up feelings onto the yellow wallpaper in her room. She eventually believes that there is a woman trapped in the wallpaper's pattern. This trapped figure symbolizes the narrator's emotional and intellectual confinement. Left with no real means of expression or escape, the narrator represses her anger and frustration and succumbs to insanity. Greg Johnson emphasizes this theme in an essay for *Studies in Short Fiction* in which he notes that the story "traces the narrator's gradual identification with her own suppressed rage, figured as a woman grasping the bars of her prison and struggling frantically to get free."

The story also addresses how physicians, specifically world-famous neurologist S. Weir Mitchell, viewed mental illness in female patients at the end of the nineteenth century. Psychologists frequently dismissed serious illnesses like depression as nothing more than hysteria or a "case of the nerves." Mitchell and his proteges advised their patients get complete bed rest, believing that intellectual activity was detrimental to women's mental health. In 1935, Gilman explained the importance of this theme in her autobiography: "The real purpose of the story was to reach Dr. S. Weir Mitchell, and convince him of the error of his ways. . . . Many years later, I met someone who said he had told them that he had changed his treatment of nervous prostration since reading 'The Yellow Wallpaper.' If that is a fact, I have not lived in vain."

Style

"The Yellow Wallpaper" tells the story of a woman's mental breakdown. Suffering from depression following the birth of her first child, the woman is taken to the country by her physician husband, where she is kept in a room decorated with yellow wallpaper that used to be a nursery. Instructed by her husband not to engage in any intellectual activity and to get total bed rest, the narrator becomes obsessed with the wallpaper until, at the end of the story, she goes insane.

Setting

"The Yellow Wallpaper" takes place in a country house that is located about three miles from the nearest village. Although the house is large and is surrounded by hedges, a garden, and servants' quarters, the narrator notes that the house and its grounds have fallen into a slight state of disrepair. At the beginning of the story, the narrator is interested in the surrounding scenery as well as the other rooms in the house. As the story progresses, however, she becomes fixated on the nursery and its yellow wallpaper. The setting has the appearance of tranquility but is actually a place of confinement—there are bars on the windows of the nursery, and the bed is secured to the floor. The isolated location of the house, its slight state of disrepair, and the narrator's further isolation in the fortress-like nursery, all symbolize the narrator's mental condition.

Topics for Further Study

- Research literature on hysteria and other "women's problems" published at the end of the 1800s and relate them to "The Yellow Wallpaper."

- What role does John feel a woman should play in society? How might a contemporary feminist view John? What are the attitudes toward acceptable roles for women today?

- Read Gilman's autobiography *The Living of Charlotte Perkins* (1935) and compare her real-life experience with depression to that of the protagonist in "The Yellow

Narration

"The Yellow Wallpaper" is an example of a first-person narrative because it is told exclusively from the viewpoint of the unnamed protagonist, and the reader is given access only to her thoughts and emotions. Since the protagonist is suffering a mental breakdown, she is also considered an unreliable narrator because the reader cannot be certain if she is accurately relating the events of the story. This adds emotional impact to the narrative because the reader is given an intimate account of the protagonist's growing feelings of despair and confusion.

The story itself is, in part, a transcription of a journal which the narrator secretly writes as she lays in bed. The writing style, and the way it changes as the story progresses, gives the reader clues to the protagonist's deteriorating mental condition. For example, throughout the story the narrator's sentences become shorter and more curt, with paragraphs consisting of only one or two sentences. This helps convey her distraught mental state and her inability to think clearly. The overall tone of the narrator's writing also changes. At the beginning of the story, she writes with humility, stating that while she does not agree with her treatment, her husband John probably knows better than she what is good for her. By the end of the narrative, however, a tone of complaint and rebellion has entered the narrator's account. When she locks the door of the nursery at the end of the story, for example, she declares: "I don't want to go out, and I don't want to have anybody come in, until John comes. I want to astonish him."

Symbolism

The most important symbol in the story is the yellow wallpaper. Most critics have concluded that the wallpaper represents the state of mind of the protagonist. In a more general sense, the wallpaper also symbolizes the way women were viewed in nineteenth-century society. It is described as containing "pointless patterns," "lame uncertain curves," and "outrageous angles" that "destroy themselves in unheard of contradictions." Despite the narrator's detailed description of the wallpaper, however, it remains mysterious. Elaine R. Hedges wrote in the afterword to the 1973 edition of the story that "the paper symbolizes [the narrator's] situation as seen by the men who control her and hence her situation as seen by herself. How can she define herself?"

Other important symbols in "The Yellow Wallpaper" are the nursery, the barred windows, and the nailed-down bed. The nursery is said to represent nineteenth-century society's tendency to view women as children, while the barred windows symbolize the emotional, social, and intellectual prison in which women of that era were kept.

Finally, the bed is said by some critics to represent repressed female sexuality.

Psychological Realism

The story is considered an example of psychological realism because it attempts to accurately portray the mental deterioration of the narrator. It is also considered realistic in that it depicts life the way it was for women during the nineteenth century. Gilman deliberately tried to make the narrator typical of that time period: she is economically dependent on her husband, she is not allowed to make her own decisions, she is discouraged from engaging in intellectual activity, and she is frequently treated like a child. Gilman also did not romanticize the character of John. While she could have depicted him sympathetically, she instead painted him as controlling, inconsiderate, and emotionally inaccessible.

Gothicism

Gilman utilizes numerous conventions of Gothic fiction in "The Yellow Wallpaper," including horror, dread, dreams, suspense, and the supernatural. For example, the story takes place on an estate, which has fallen into a state of disrepair, three miles from the nearest village. This sense of isolation is frequently used in Gothic stories to create a foreboding tone. The narrator is also struck with the "strangeness" and "ghostliness" of the place. E. Suzanne Owens argues in *Haunting the*

House of Fiction that "to a reader familiar with the Gothic, the events of the story suggest possession as much as they do hallucination."

Historical Context

"The Yellow Wallpaper" was written and published in 1892. The last three decades of the nineteenth century comprised a period of growth, development, and expansion for the United States. Following the Civil War, which ended in 1865, the United States entered the era of Reconstruction, which lasted until 1877. There were many social and cultural changes during this period. Charles Darwin's *The Origin of Species* (1892) expounded his theory of evolution, and further incited controversy over women's roles and issues. His theory of evolution flouted conventional wisdom, contending that women were actually the hardier and more necessary sex, the one able to preserve the species. Because women were mothers, they were vital to survival. Darwin's theory was used to promote both sides of what came to be known as the "Woman Question." Some scientists argued that because women were physiologically hardier, they were capable of being both mothers and professionals. Others contended that Darwin's theory proved that motherhood was necessary to women and that it should retain a supreme priority in a woman's life.

Throughout much of the 1800s, the common law doctrine of *femme convert* was prevalent in the United States. Under this law, wives were property of their husbands and had no direct legal control over their earnings, children, or belongings. Some state laws prohibited women from going into business without their husband's consent, and some dictated that a husband could decide where the family would live. Other state laws dictated that adultery was not considered sufficient grounds for divorce if committed by a man, but it was if committed by the wife. Women also could not vote; they were not allowed to do so until 1920, when the 19th Amendment to the Constitution was adopted. In 1875, in *Minor* v. *Happensett*, the Supreme Court ruled that states could withhold the right to vote from women as they did from criminals and the mentally insane. The rise of women's consciousness regarding such oppression was influenced by their participation in the abolitionist movement prior to and during the Civil War. In 1869, the first organizations devoted to women's rights were founded. By 1890, such organizations claimed a total of 500,000 members. While there were more women than men in high school by 1890, higher education was not an option for most women, and the only professions open to them were nursing and elementary education.

Compare & Contrast

- **1892:** Women cannot vote for public officials or hold public office. Occupations other than teaching, nursing, low-level factory labor, or domestic service are closed to them, and a college education is rare.
  Today: Women have achieved a

great deal toward true equality with men. Virtually all occupations are now open to women. Many issues remain, however, including equal pay.

- **1890s:** A rash of so called "hysteria" cases occur during the late 1800s and early 1900s. Medical professionals define the malady in terms of femininity and female sexuality, claiming that women are prone to hysteria because of their emotionality and delicate constitutions.

  Today: Hysteria has long been considered an invalid diagnosis of mental illness. Post-partum depression is recognized as a common condition and can be treated in a variety of ways, often with medication.

- **1890s:** Along with Gilman, Kate Chopin, Louisa May Alcott, and Sarah Orne Jewett are some of the few women writers who obtain success and popularity by publishing their stories in women's magazines.

  Today: Many women writers are being rediscovered and reevaluated, such as Gilman, and have been added to the literary cannon.

Gilman, as a leading feminist and social activist during the late nineteenth century, argued that women's secondary status in society, and especially women's economic dependence on men, was not the result of biological inferiority but rather of culturally enforced behavior. In "The Yellow Wallpaper," which was, in part, a reaction to the oppression of women prevalent during this time, Gilman emphasized these beliefs. In 1926, she stated, regarding her work in general, "One girl reads this, and takes fire! Her life is changed. She becomes a power—a mover of others—I write for her."

Critical Overview

"The Yellow Wallpaper," which was first published in the *New England Magazine* in 1892 after being rejected by the editor of *The Atlantic*, did not receive much serious attention until American writer and critic William Dean Howells published it in his *The Great Modern American Stories* in 1920. In that volume he wrote: "Now that I have it in my collection, I shiver over it as much as I did when I first read it in manuscript, though I agree with the editor of *The Atlantic* of the time that it was too terribly good to be printed." It was not until 1973, when it was republished after being out of print for years, that the first lengthy analysis of the story was written by Elaine R. Hedges. Writing in the afterword to the volume, she stated that "The Yellow Wallpaper' is a small literary masterpiece" and a work that "does deserve the widest possible audience."

Since then, "The Yellow Wallpaper" has received widespread critical attention. Contemporary scholars have interpreted the story in numerous ways, with feminist readings being the most common. Reviewers focus on the relationship between the narrator and her husband John, maintaining that John's treatment of his wife represents the power-lessness and repression of women during the late nineteenth-century. Hedges concluded that the story is "one of the rare pieces of literature we have by a nineteenth-century woman which directly confronts the sexual politics of the male-female, husband-wife relationship."

Critics have also commented on the story's focus on psychology and its influence as an example of both psychological realism and Gothic fiction. It is often considered one of the most detailed and emotionally charged accounts of depression and despair in short fiction because it is told from the vantage point of the person actually suffering a nervous breakdown. Furthermore, Gilman does not romanticize or downplay the realities of mental suffering. In addition to being discussed as feminist literature and as an example of psychological realism, "The Yellow Wallpaper" has been lauded as a preeminent piece of Gothic fiction because of its incorporation of such Gothic literary elements as horror, suspense, and the supernatural.

"The Yellow Wallpaper," like Gilman's other short stories, has been faulted by some critics who claim the story is nothing more than a vehicle through which she explicated her feminist social beliefs. In fact, Gilman once stated that she wrote the story "to preach. If it is literature, that just happened." However, most critics have acknowledged that "The Yellow Wallpaper" is realistic, accessible, and thought-provoking and have called it Gilman's best work of fiction.

What Do I Read Next?

- The short story "The Tell-Tale Heart" (1843) by Edgar Allan Poe is told from the perspective of an insane man who murders an old man and buries the dismembered body beneath the floor boards of the room in which he lives.

- In her nonfiction work *Women and Economics* (1898), Gilman argues that men and women are more similar than different and that women should have all of the social and economic freedoms of men, including the right to work.

- In *The Treatment of Certain Forms of Neurasthenia and Hysteria* (1887), doctor S. Weir Mitchell explains his treatment of nervous prostration in women. He advocates a "rest-cure," or complete bed rest, believing that intellectual, literary, and artistic pursuits are destructive to women's mental health.

- The short story "Silent Snow, Secret Snow" (1932) by American writer Conrad Aiken explores the hallucinations of a sensitive youngster named Paul Haslemann.

- *The Madwomen in the Attic* (1979) by Susan Gubar and Sandra Gilbert examines the ways nineteenth-century women writers, including Gilman and Charlotte Bronte, expressed forbidden emotions in their works.

- *The Awakening* (1899) is a novel by American writer Kate Chopin. It is the story of a conventional wife and mother who, after engaging in an extramarital affair, commits suicide when she realizes she cannot reconcile her actions with the moral restrictions of society.

Sources

Gilbert, Sandra M., and Susan Gubar. "Infection in the Sentence: The Woman Writer and the Anxiety of Authorship," in *The Madwoman in the Attic: The Woman Writer and the Nineteenth-Century Literary Imagination*, Yale University Press, 1979, pp. 45-92.

Hedges, Elaine R. An afterword to *The Yellow Wallpaper*, by Charlotte Perkins Gilman, Feminist Press, 1973, pp. 37-63.

Howells, William Dean. "A Reminiscent Introduction," in *The Great Modern American Stories: An Anthology*, Boni and Liveright, 1920, pp. vii-xiv.

Owens, E. Suzanne. "The Ghostly Double behind the Wallpaper in Charlotte Perkins Gilman's 'The Yellow Wallpaper'," in *Haunting the House of Fiction: Feminist Perspectives on Ghost Stories by American Women*, University of Tennessee Press, 1991, pp. 64-79.

Further Reading

Golden, Catherine. "'Overwriting' the Rest Cure: Charlotte Perkins Gilman's Literary Escape from S. Weir Mitchell's Fictionalization of Women," in *Critical Essays on Charlotte Perkins Gilman*, edited by Joanne B. Karpinski, G. K. Hall, 1992, pp. 144-58.

>Golden examines the relationships between Mitchell's rest cure, Gilman's fiction and nineteenth-century women.

Hedges, Elaine R. "Out at Last?: 'The Yellow Wallpaper' after Two Decades of Feminist Criticism," in *Critical Essays on Charlotte Perkins Gilman*, edited by Joanne B. Karpinski, G. K. Hall, 1992, pp. 222-33.

>Hedges provides an overview of feminist criticism of "The Yellow Wallpaper" since the story's rediscovery in the 1970s.

Jacobus, Mary. "An Unnecessary Maze of Sign-Readings," in *Reading Woman: Essays in Feminist Criticism*, Columbia University Press, 1986, pp. 229-48.

>Jacobus discusses the validity of Freudian and feminist readings of the story.

Karpinski, Joanne B. An introduction to *Critical*

Essays on Charlotte Perkins Gilman, edited by Joanne B. Karpinski, G. K. Hall & Co., 1992, pp. 1-16.

> Karpinski discusses Gilman's life and work and provides a brief introduction to the articles included in the volume.

Lane, Ann J. *To Herland and Beyond*, Penguin, 1991, 413 p.

> This biography of Gilman provides detailed information about the author's life as well as her writings.

Shumaker, Conrad. "Too Terribly Good to Be Printed": Charlotte Gilman's "The Yellow Wallpaper," in *American Literature*, Vol. 57, no. 4, 1985, pp. 588-99.

> Shumaker presents a reading of "The Yellow Wallpaper" in the context of the treatment of women in the nineteenth century.

Shumaker, Conrad. "Realism, Reform, and the Audience: Charlotte Perkins Gilman's Unreadable Wallpaper," in *Arizona Quarterly*, Vol. 47, no. 1, spring, 1991, pp. 81-93.

> Discussion of the elements of realism and reform in "The Yellow Wallpaper."

CPSIA information can be obtained
at www.ICGtesting.com
Printed in the USA
BVHW030009100922
646660BV00014B/1540

9 781375 396691